The Handmaid's Tale

Lightbox Literature Studies

Valerie Weber and Katie Gillespie

LIGHTBOX
openlightbox.com

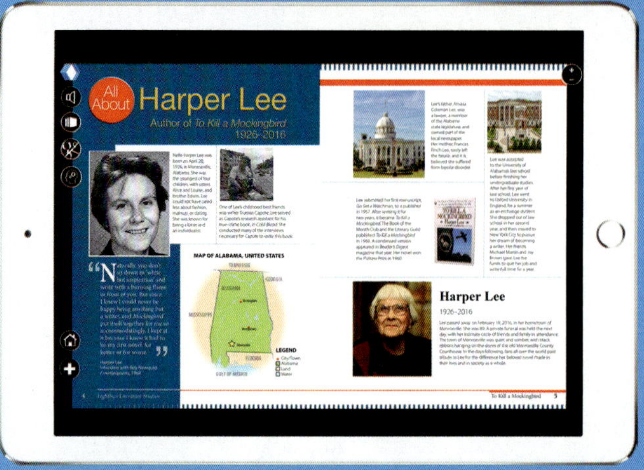

Lightbox is an all-inclusive digital solution for the teaching and learning of curriculum topics in an original, groundbreaking way. Lightbox is based on National Curriculum Standards.

STANDARD FEATURES OF LIGHTBOX

AUDIO High-quality narration using text-to-speech system

VIDEOS Embedded high-definition video clips

ACTIVITIES Printable PDFs that can be emailed and graded

WEBLINKS Curated links to external, child-safe resources

SLIDESHOWS Pictorial overviews of key concepts

TRANSPARENCIES Step-by-step layering of maps, diagrams, charts, and timelines

INTERACTIVE MAPS Interactive maps and aerial satellite imagery

QUIZZES Ten multiple choice questions that are automatically graded and emailed for teacher assessment

KEY WORDS Matching key concepts to their definitions

MORE Extra information and details on the subject

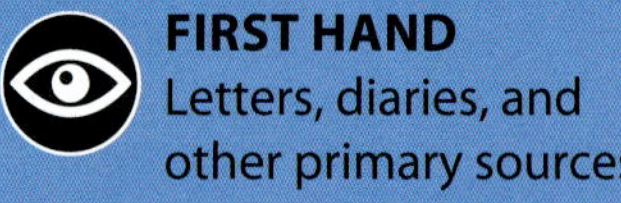
FIRST HAND Letters, diaries, and other primary sources

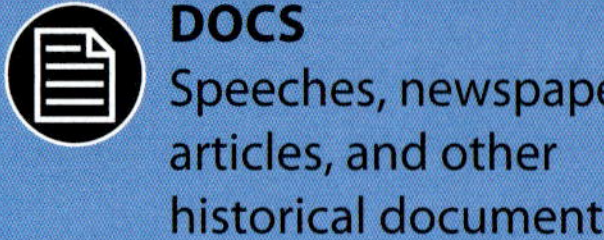
DOCS Speeches, newspaper articles, and other historical documents

Contents

MARGARET ATWOOD
The Handmaid's Tale
Shortlisted for the Booker Prize

RUBRIC

Conducting an Interview

Students will conduct an interview with a community member about a time period in their community's history, and submit an audio recording and transcript of the interview. An exemplary interview will meet the following criteria.

- Clearly defines the purpose of the interview
- Conducts thorough background research to inform the focus of the interview and the questions
- Drafts a complete list of thoughtful, in-depth, and varied questions prior to the interview
- Interviews a subject with relevant knowledge on the topic and time period in question
- Asks questions in a logical order, building upon each other
- Treats the interview subject in a polite, respectful, and professional manner
- Does not interrupt or rush the interview subject
- Shows interest and enthusiasm in responses and follow-up questions
- Chooses follow-up questions that demonstrate active listening
- Asks for clarification and further details when necessary
- Asks questions about personal experiences related to the topic
- Asks questions regarding factual information and the interview subject's opinion on the topic
- Asks creative questions that reflect fresh insights on the topic
- Records the full interview in a quiet environment
- Organizes and edits the interview transcript to be clear and factual

Margaret Atwood

Author of *The Handmaid's Tale*

1939–

Margaret Atwood was born on November 18, 1939, in Ottawa, Ontario, Canada. She spent much of her childhood with her older brother in the wilderness of northern Quebec and north of Lake Superior. Her father worked as an **entomologist**. He built one of the family's homes in the woods for his studies. The Atwood children were homeschooled by their mother, a former nutritionist. They ate fish from the nearby lake as well as animals caught in the woods. After her studies were complete, Atwood roamed the woods freely. With heavy pants tucked into her socks to avoid insect bites, she examined nature closely. In cold weather, the children created their own comic books.

> "Stories about the future always have a 'what-if' premise, and *The Handmaid's Tale* has several. For instance: if you wanted to seize power in the U.S., abolish liberal democracy and set up a dictatorship,...[w]hat would be your cover story? It would not resemble any form of communism or socialism: those would be too unpopular. It might use the name of democracy as an excuse for abolishing liberal democracy... Nations never build apparently radical forms of government on foundations that aren't there already."
>
> Margaret Atwood,
> "Haunted by *The Handmaid's Tale*,"
> *The Guardian*
> January 20, 2012

MAP OF CANADA AND THE UNITED STATES

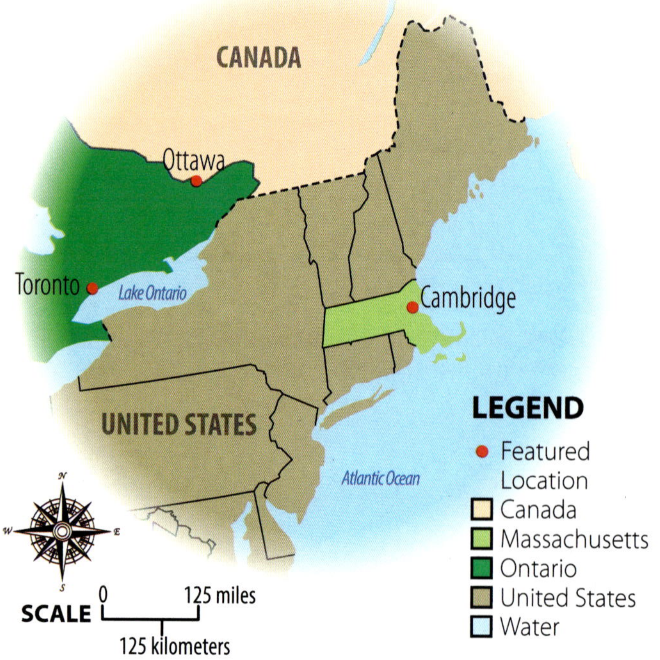

In 1946, Atwood's father started teaching at the University of Toronto, and the family moved to the city. Atwood found herself surrounded by kids focused on popular culture and clothing, topics she knew little about. She later told an interviewer, "I wasn't in the wilderness when I was 16, I was in high school. Some people think of that as the wilderness." While in high school, Atwood decided she wanted to become a writer.

After graduating from the University of Toronto, Atwood began graduate studies at Radcliffe, where she received a Master's degree. She went on to Harvard University in Boston, but never finished her Ph.D. program there. Instead, she started publishing her poetry. Her first pamphlet was published in 1961. At the same time, she was teaching English at various universities in Canada.

Atwood's work has included larger books of poetry, novels, short fiction, children's books, and graphic novels. She has written academic treatises that have shaped how the world views Canadian fiction, as well as television and radio scripts. Atwood does not like the term "science fiction" applied to her works that are set in the future. She prefers the term "speculative fiction," since she takes events, cultural trends, and attitudes, and draws out their future consequences.

Atwood continues to write, lecture, and give interviews. She has lived in Toronto, Ontario, consistently since 1992, along with her partner, the novelist Graeme Gibson. Atwood is an environmental activist as well as a fundraiser, primarily for conservation and literacy-related causes. She gave cameo performances in the Hulu adaptation of *The Handmaid's Tale* and the Netflix adaptation of *Alias Grace*. Atwood always keeps her next writing project a secret from the public.

ACTIVITIES

Google Maps

Harvard University, Cambridge, Massachusetts

Explore the university campus Margaret Atwood once attended using street view. The city of Cambridge is also the setting of the novel's fictional Republic of Gilead.

First Hand

Margaret Atwood on why 'The Handmaid's Tale' is more relevant now than ever

Examine this interview with Margaret Atwood from the *Los Angeles Times*.

1. What types of questions does the interviewer ask? What topics does she focus on? Why would she focus on these specific areas?
2. The interviewer notes that although *The Handmaid's Tale* has been a banned book, it is also found on required reading lists. Why do you think this is the case? In what ways might this fact have impacted the way the book and its messages are perceived?

RUBRIC

Researching for a Writing Assignment

Students will complete a thorough research process to prepare for a writing assignment, and organize their research in a logical manner that supports their writing. An exemplary research process will meet the following criteria.

- Creates a goal for the research, based on the topic and working thesis
- Creates specific, thoughtful, and inventive research questions that are relevant to the topic of the writing assignment
- Produces a list of categories, key words, and related ideas to effectively assist in researching
- Uses high-quality sources that pertain to the topic and come in a variety of formats, such as books, journals, primary sources, websites, and databases
- Determines accuracy of all sources
- Uses sources that provide balanced research and various perspectives on the topic in question
- Takes notes to highlight the key facts and ideas in order to answer all research questions
- Extracts relevant, detailed information from the sources during the note-taking process
- Organizes the research notes in a clear and concise manner
- Organizes the research notes logically and in a way that sets up the information and ideas for analysis and the writing process
- Analyzes the information and produces ideas and points to support the working thesis
- Uses an effective and suitable format to present all research
- Properly cites all sources used

Setting of the Novel

Atwood set *The Handmaid's Tale* in the near future, in an unknown place. She gives hints about the location throughout the novel, and readers must pick up clues to the larger setting. The town once held a university. Its walls have become known as "The Wall," where bodies now hang. The narrator, Offred, and her companion, Ofglen, visit a large, old building once called Memorial Hall. The town must be old, since it also holds a church erected hundreds of years ago.

Snapshot

In **1980**, the population of **Cambridge** was about **95,300**. As of **2016**, it was **110,650**.

In **1985**, women in the United States earned an average of **64.6** cents for every dollar that men earned. By **2015**, women's earnings had only risen to **79.6** cents for every dollar that men earned.

In **1985**, the national **birthrate** in the United States was **15.8** babies **per 1,000 people**. By **2016**, the birthrate had declined to **12.4 babies per 1,000 people**.

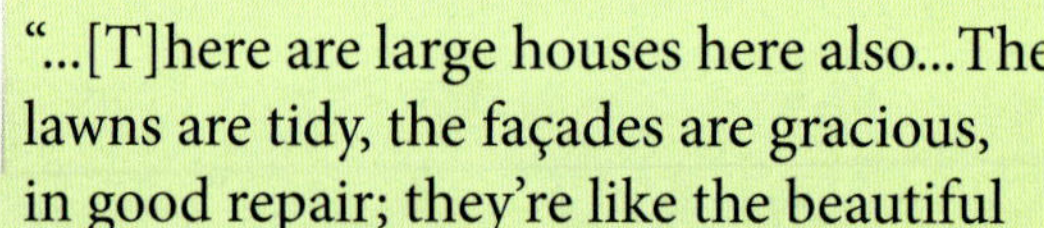

Gilead

"...[T]here are large houses here also...The lawns are tidy, the façades are gracious, in good repair; they're like the beautiful pictures they used to print in the magazines about homes and gardens and interior decoration. There is the same absence of people, the same air of being asleep. The street is almost like a museum, or a street in a model town constructed to show the way people used to live. As in those pictures, those museums, those model towns, there are no children. This is the heart of Gilead..."

Offred, Chapter Five

In interviews, Atwood admits that the novel's setting is Cambridge, where she attended Harvard University from 1962 to 1963, and again from 1965 to 1967. Her ancestors, who were Puritans, were from the area. They arrived there from Great Britain. One of her ancestors was hanged, charged with being a witch. However, the hanging did not succeed, and the woman lived. Atwood justifies her choice of setting: "You often hear in North America, 'It can't happen here,' but it happened quite early on. The Puritans banished people who didn't agree with them, so we would be rather smug to assume that the seeds are not there. That's why I set the book in Cambridge."

Offred describes places in the city while reviewing her memories. Settings include the Commander's House, her dorm room, her apartment during her university days, and her first apartment with her then-partner, Luke. The Rachel and Leah Re-education Center, or Red Center, which turns fertile individual women into anonymous handmaids, has taken over a gym. Offred's current setting is strictly controlled. For the most part, she must stay in a single room. She is only allowed out in town if she is with another Handmaid, or with a Guardian, one of the soldiers of Gilead. The Commander breaks the law by taking her to Jezebel's.

ACTIVITIES

Video

The Handmaids Tale Part 1: Crash Course Literature #403
Find out more about Atwood's dystopian Republic of Gilead by watching this video.

1. In the video, John Green claims that "in contemporary life, we expect progress in the future." However, instead of such progress, he says that *The Handmaid's Tale* shows "one vision of what can happen when yearning for the future takes the form of grasping for the past." What do you think he means by these assertions? Do you agree or disagree with John's claims? Give reasons for your answer.
2. Why do you think Atwood chose to open the novel in the Rachel and Leah Re-education Center? How does Offred's description of it affect the reader's understanding of her situation and that of the other handmaidens?

Weblink

What Does Gilead Mean In 'The Handmaid's Tale'?
Learn more about the roots of Gilead's name by reading this article.

1. Why do you think Atwood chose the name Gilead for the setting of *The Handmaid's Tale*? What effect does this have on the reader? Explain why you think so.
2. What is the connection between the Republic of Gilead and the Bible story of Rachel and Jacob?
3. What parallels can you draw between the Handmaids in Atwood's novel and Bilhah, the Handmaid of Rachel and Jacob?

Time Period of the Novel

The Handmaid's Tale takes place in the not-too-distant future. A religious group, inspired by the Bible, and reacting to widespread environmental disasters and infertility, has taken over much of the United States. They call their new nation Gilead, after a place in the Bible. Gilead also goes back to the times of the Puritans, who came to North America to establish their own political system. The Puritans thought of themselves as a people chosen by God to live godly lives. They were supposed to follow strict moral guidelines.

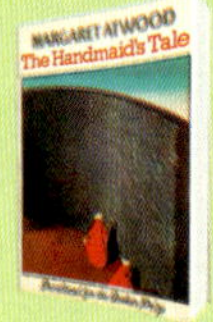

The End of Freedom

"I guess that's how they were able to do it, in the way they did, all at once, without anyone knowing beforehand. If there had still been portable money, it would have been more difficult.

It was after the catastrophe, when they shot the President and machine-gunned the Congress and the army declared a state of emergency. They blamed it on the Islamic fanatics at the time...

I was stunned. Everyone was, I know that. It was hard to believe. The entire government, gone like that. How did they get in, how did it happen?

That was when they suspended the Constitution. They said it would be temporary. There wasn't even any rioting in the streets. People stayed home at night, watching television, looking for some direction. There wasn't even an enemy you could put your finger on."

Offred, Chapter Twenty-Eight

In Atwood's Gilead, women are fired from their jobs without cause, and their bank accounts are closed for no reason. Assigned to categories based on their fertility, women become Handmaids, domestic servants, and "econowives." Men also have specific roles to play, as Commanders, soldiers, spies, and workers. Television news focuses on the new regime's efforts to take over more of the United States. Other Christian sects, such as the Quakers and the Baptists, are now the enemy.

Atwood began writing *The Handmaid's Tale* in West Berlin, a divided German city, in 1984. She had grown up during World War II and knew that governments could suddenly change. Atwood based her novel on events before and during the 1980s. The idea of handmaids bearing children for the powerful comes from the Bible. In it, an **infertile** woman named Rachel tells her husband, Jacob, "Behold my maid Bilhah, go in unto her; and she shall bear upon my knees, that I may also have children by her."

In the 1970s, a military coup overthrew the democratic government of Argentina. The generals imposed censorship and strict curfews, and increased the power of the secret police. They took the children of political prisoners and raised them as their own. In Romania, the government issued a decree that prevented women from controlling their own reproductive health. Until the mid-1970s, women in the United States could not get a credit card without a man to cosign for it. During the 1980s, religious groups such as the Moral Majority were becoming more politically active in the United States. They advocated a return to so-called traditional values, working against women's rights and gay rights. Atwood wove these events and others into a fictional place and time.

ACTIVITIES

Video

Why should you read "The Handmaid's Tale"? - Naomi R. Mercer

Discover some of the real-life events that inspired Atwood's creation of Gilead by watching this video.

1. In the video, Naomi R. Mercer points out that "although *The Handmaid's Tale* is set in the future, one of Atwood's self-imposed rules in writing it was that she wouldn't use any event or practice that hadn't already happened in human history." Do you find this fact surprising? Why or why not? How does the knowledge that Atwood imposed this rule upon the writing of the novel affect your interpretation it?
2. How did the time period that *The Handmaid's Tale* was written in impact Atwood's creation of the novel? In what ways might the story be different if it were written today?

Weblink

The real-life events that inspired The Handmaid's Tale

Review the *Stylist* article by Kayleigh Dray about the historical events that Atwood drew on when writing *The Handmaid's Tale*.

1. In the article, a parallel is drawn between the way women are treated in *The Handmaid's Tale* and the way Jewish people were treated in Nazi Germany. Do you think this is a reasonable comparison? Why or why not?
2. During the events leading up to the Republic of Gilead, the people did not wake up. Dray says this "calls to mind the events leading up to the Holocaust." What are the similarities between these events? Give specific examples.

RUBRIC

Writing a Short Story

Students will choose an excerpt from the novel and use it as their inspiration in writing a short story. An exemplary short story will meet the following criteria.

- Engages the reader from the opening line
- Establishes a clear, consistent point of view
- Introduces a narrator and a setting
- Develops an engaging conflict at the heart of the narrative to build tension and keep the reader interested
- Develops characters and events through purposeful and well-crafted literary devices
- Creates a logical progression of events in the narrative that build upon each other using various techniques
- Explores ideas, concepts, and writing styles with creativity and originality
- Demonstrates a high level of skill in using appropriate narrative techniques to tell the story
- Concludes the narrative in a thoughtful, effective manner appropriate to the narrative
- Uses varied, purposeful diction and syntax to affect style and serve the narrative
- Writes with clarity, imagination, and a unique, personal voice
- Does not use stereotypes or clichés
- Uses effective, believable dialogue
- Uses correct spelling, grammar, and punctuation

Conflict in the Novel

In literature, conflict is a struggle between two or more opposing forces, creating tension that must be resolved. This is the main challenge that the protagonist, or main character, faces throughout the story. This struggle is often between the protagonist and antagonist, but there are other types of conflict found in literature. Conflicts can be internal, within the protagonist, or external, with someone or something else. Conflict is a vital element in any work of fiction. Without it, the story does not move forward.

MAN VS. MAN

In external conflicts, such as man versus man, characters conflict verbally in arguments or physically in fights. In *Lord of the Flies*, Jack and Ralph struggle for leadership of a group of boys stranded on an island. Ralph wants an orderly, democratic, and civil society. Jack has no respect for Ralph or his ideas, and forms his own tribe to try to kill Ralph and his followers.

MAN VS. SELF

Internal conflicts involve characters struggling with themselves. They often feel two opposing emotions or desires, and the story focuses on how this struggle is resolved. In *Divergent*, Tris lives in a **dystopian** society in which people are divided into categories. While she grew up with her family in one category, she must decide which category she wants to join.

MAN VS. SOCIETY

In a man versus society conflict, a character's morals and values conflict with those of society. *The Giver* is set in a seemingly **utopian** community in which people do not remember their pasts or have choices about their own futures. Jonas is charged with remembering the positive and negative experiences of life. He does not want the community to go on without memories or choices, and rebels against it.

MAN VS. NATURE

Characters pitted against nature often learn something about themselves or the world in the process. Nature may be as small as a garden or as big as a landscape. In *Into the Wild*, Christopher McCandless rejects society, as embodied by his parents. He enters the Alaskan wilderness nearly unprepared to live off the land.

Types of Conflict in *The Handmaid's Tale*

The two main conflicts in *The Handmaid's Tale* are man versus society and man versus man.

Man versus Society

"If it's a story I'm telling, then I have control over the ending. Then there will be an ending, to the story, and real life will come after it. I can pick up where I left off.
It isn't a story I'm telling.
It's also a story I'm telling, in my head, as I go along. Tell rather than write, because I have nothing to write with and writing is in any case forbidden. But if it's a story, even in my head, I must be telling it to someone. You don't tell a story only to yourself. There's always someone else.
Even when there is no one."

Offred, Chapter Seven

Offred

Man versus Man

"I want to see as little of you as possible, she said. I expect you feel the same way about me.
I didn't answer, as a yes would have been insulting, a no contradictory.
I know you aren't stupid, she went on. She inhaled, blew out the smoke. I've read your file. As far as I'm concerned, this is like a business transaction. But if I get trouble, I'll give trouble back. You understand?
Yes, Ma'am, I said.
Don't call me Ma'am, she said irritably. You're not a Martha.
I didn't ask what I was supposed to call her, because I could see that she hoped I would never have the occasion to call her anything at all... But I could see already that I wouldn't have liked her, nor she me."

Offred, Chapter Three

ACTIVITIES

 **More**

The Types of Conflict in *The Handmaid's Tale*
Analyze the excerpts from the novel revealing the types of conflict as they appear in *The Handmaid's Tale*.

1. How do these excerpts of conflict reveal the novel's theme? How do they reveal character? Explain and defend your ideas.
2. Write an analysis of Atwood's development of conflict between Offred and Serena Joy. What deeper truths may be suggested about these characters as a result of their conflict?

Document

The Handmaid's Tale by Margaret Atwood: examining its utopian, dystopian, feminist and postmodernist traditions
Review the thesis by Angela Michelle Gulick of Iowa State University, exploring Atwood's novel.

1. Who do you think is the intended audience for this document? Why? Are the tone and language used appropriate for this audience? Explain your answer.
2. What are the main points of the document and how are they presented? Are these points conveyed effectively to the reader? Why or why not?

RUBRIC

Holding a Classroom Debate

Students will form groups and prepare arguments for a debate on a controversial issue. Exemplary performance in a debate will meet the following criteria.

- Demonstrates in-depth understanding of the topic and related information
- Presents strong, logical, and convincing arguments
- Communicates in a clear and confident manner
- Maintains eye contact
- Uses clear vocal tone and a reasonable rate of vocal delivery
- Uses respectful and appropriate language and body language
- Delivers arguments, evidence, and counter-evidence in an engaging and persuasive manner
- Supports each major point of an argument with several relevant and detailed facts and examples
- Connects all arguments to the overall topic in a clear, concise, and organized manner
- Presents the arguments and supporting evidence in a clear, logical manner
- Presents clear, thorough, and accurate information throughout the debate
- Addresses all of the opposing team's arguments with counter-arguments
- Identifies any weakness in the opposing team's arguments
- Constructs strong and relevant counter-arguments using accurate information
- Presents strong and persuasive arguments throughout the debate
- Summarizes the arguments in the closing statement

Introducing the Characters

Characters act, move, decide, and talk to and interact with other characters. Even thinking is an act. Through an author's descriptions of the characters and their actions, the reader comes to know them as individuals.

Major Characters in *The Handmaid's Tale*

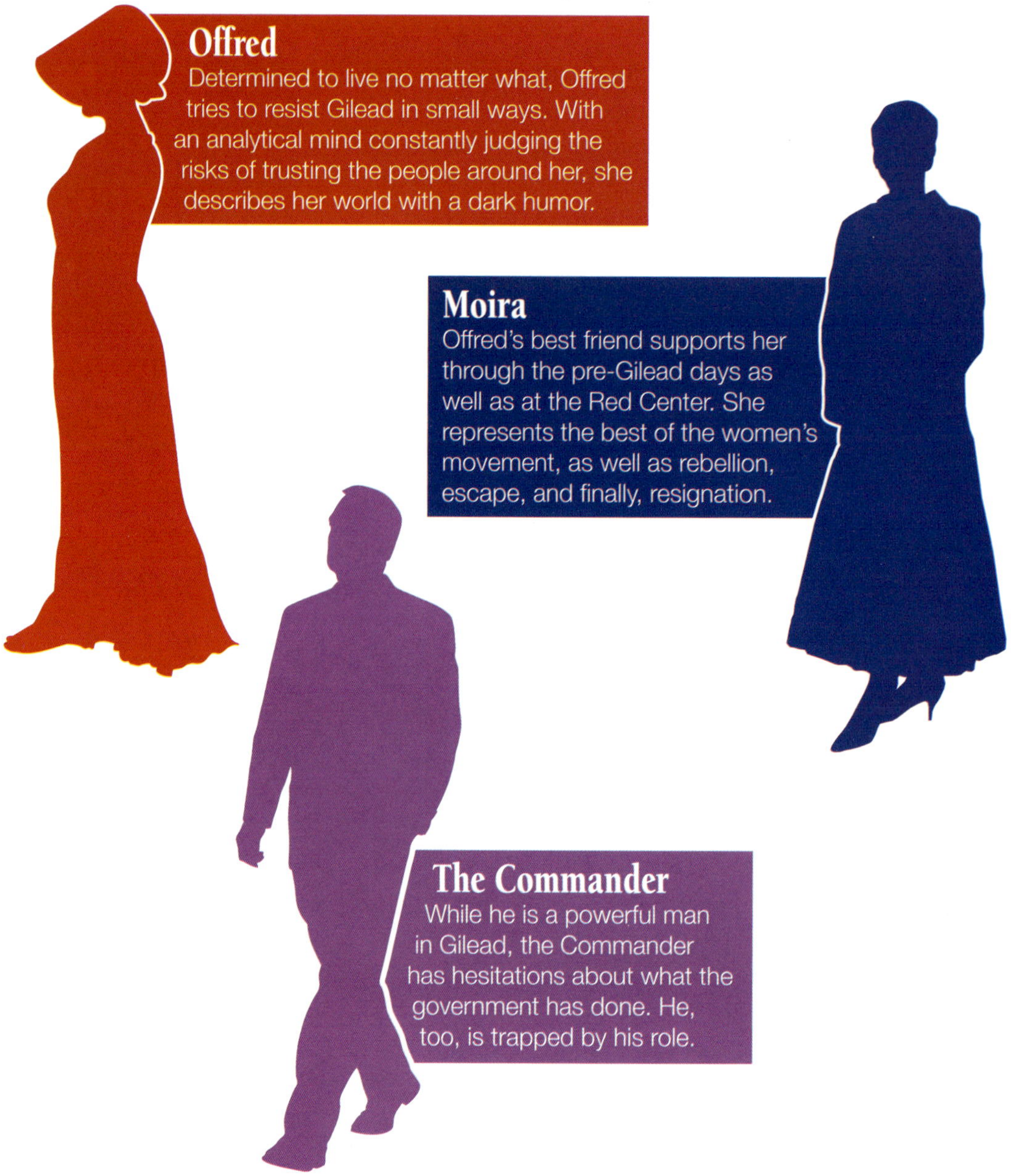

Offred

Determined to live no matter what, Offred tries to resist Gilead in small ways. With an analytical mind constantly judging the risks of trusting the people around her, she describes her world with a dark humor.

Moira

Offred's best friend supports her through the pre-Gilead days as well as at the Red Center. She represents the best of the women's movement, as well as rebellion, escape, and finally, resignation.

The Commander

While he is a powerful man in Gilead, the Commander has hesitations about what the government has done. He, too, is trapped by his role.

The protagonist in *The Handmaid's Tale* is also the narrator. Since Offred is the narrator, readers do not know her through the author's description, but instead, know her primarily through her own actions. Offred's character is revealed through her flashbacks. Atwood has presented a number of antagonists, including Aunt Elizabeth and Aunt Lydia, Serena Joy, and the even more threatening characters of Gilead's leaders and their henchmen.

The other characters in *The Handmaid's Tale* are known primarily through Offred's depiction and evaluation of their actions. While the reader knows only a few details of the narrator's physical appearance, Offred herself gives clear descriptions of others'. Serena Joy is described both in her life before Gilead and as the Commander's wife. According to Offred, Nick "has a French face, lean, whimsical, all planes and angles, with creases around the mouth..."

Many different types of minor characters assist in moving the plot forward. A dynamic character, such as Moira, changes throughout the story, usually after facing conflict. A static character, such as Aunt Lydia, does not undergo changes. A flat character, such as Rita, has few distinguishing personality traits, while a rounded character, such as the Commander, has a more complex personality.

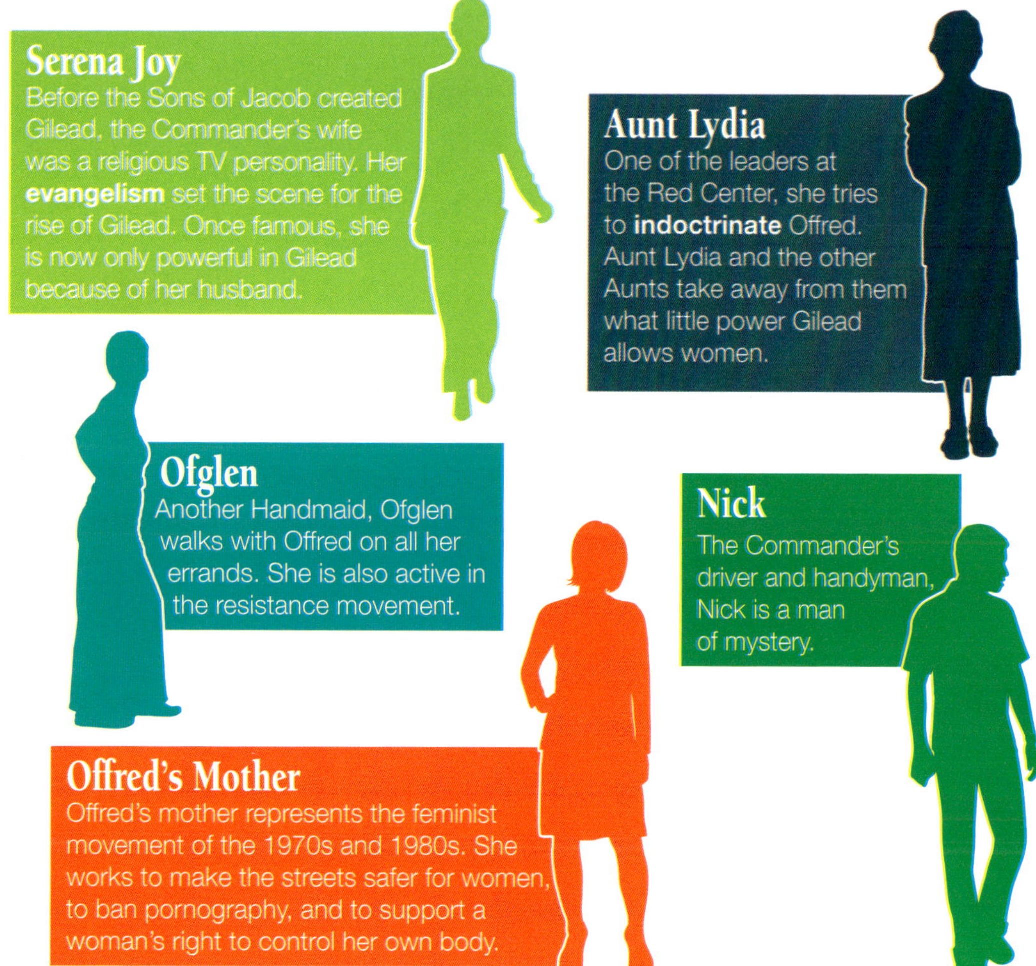

ACTIVITIES

Weblink

Character Analysis of the Commander

Review a character analysis of the Commander and debate his role in *The Handmaid's Tale*.

1. Why does the Commander pose an ethical problem for Offred? How does this affect the reader's opinion of him? Give textual evidence to support your claims.
2. Do you think the Commander is an agent of oppression or a prisoner of Gilead's structures? Is it possible for him to fall into both categories? Why or why not?

More

Character Development in *The Handmaid's Tale*

Analyze the characters in *The Handmaid's Tale* using the descriptions on the character map and excerpts from each character. Then, choose a character and answer the following questions.

1. Which of the writer's techniques are most effective at revealing this character's traits? Why?
2. In what ways is the characterization of this character ineffective? What could be done to improve this character's function in the novel? Defend your ideas with evidence.

RUBRIC

Creating a Literary Device Analysis Booklet

Students will analyze the author's use of a literary device in the novel, and create a booklet to present this analysis. An exemplary literary device analysis booklet will meet the following criteria.

- Defines the chosen literary device accurately and in detail
- Places the definition of the literary device at the beginning of the booklet
- Provides strong, specific examples of how this literary device is used in the novel
- Describes examples in detail, with quotations properly integrated
- Includes thorough analysis of the use, purpose, and effectiveness of each example of how the chosen literary device is used in the novel
- Arranges all pages logically
- Examples are organized chronologically
- Provides no more than one example and its analysis per page
- Creates a neat, well-organized, and attractive booklet
- Booklet is colorful and displays the student's creativity
- Uses illustrations to represent the chosen literary device and the examples of how it is used in the novel

The Art of Storytelling

Storytelling is a way to entertain, engage with others, teach, or communicate perspectives on society. A narrative, or story, is a series of events that is often logically arranged. When writing his or her story, a writer structures the narrative in a particular way. The writer can also use different types of literary devices to create a distinct style and to convey the narrative's overall message. Atwood paints a picture of society with words and stories. She layers on the details throughout the novel.

Structure of a Narrative

Each narrative has a structure, which writers keep in mind when creating a story. The most common narrative structure, known as dramatic structure or Freytag's Pyramid, consists of five main components, which are all used in *The Handmaid's Tale*.

Freytag's Pyramid

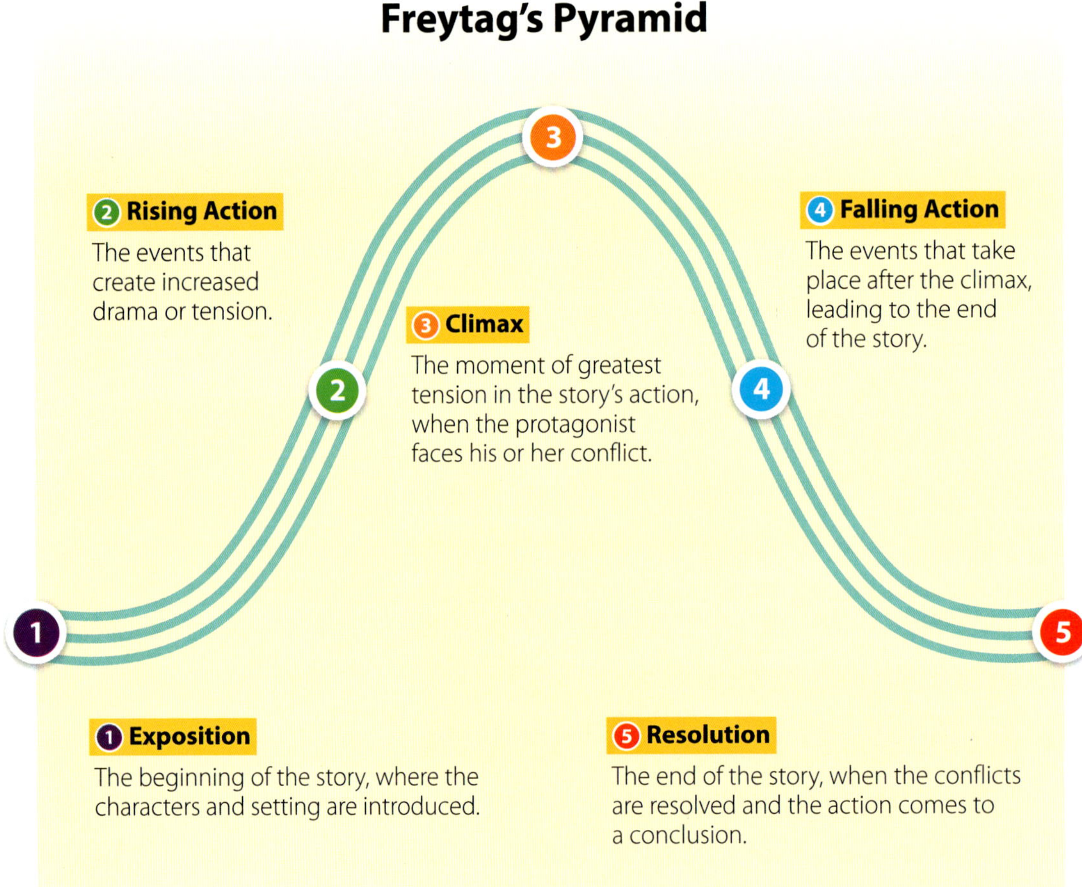

Plot

A plot is the sequence in which the story's events unfold. These events build on each other and are organized in a logical manner. Atwood has created a difficult plot to follow in that the narrator does not present her story in **chronological** order. Instead, Offred describes both her current circumstances and memories of the past. The reader must follow as her narrative skips around in time.

Plot Points in Chapter Thirteen of *The Handmaid's Tale*

1. Offred contemplates boredom and its purpose in both pre-Gilead and Gilead times.
2. She does her exercises to fend off boredom.
3. Offred remembers her naps and exhaustion from drugs in the food at the Red Center.
4. She thinks about seeing Moira enter the Red Center and their brief conversation on a walk.
5. Offred listens to Janine's description of being attacked and shares in blaming Janine.
6. Offred meets with Moira in the bathroom.
7. Offred remembers her first apartment and Luke.
8. She dreams of trying to escape Gilead with her daughter and their eventual capture.

Literary Devices

Literary devices are specific tools that create more compelling stories. Writers use these devices to add depth, meaning, insight, and suspense to their stories. The two types of literary devices are literary elements and literary techniques.

ACTIVITIES

Weblink

7 Tips for Writers from Margaret Atwood
Examine some of Atwood's advice about writing.

1. Atwood claims that "[w]hat you read is as important as what you write." Why do you think she believes this to be true? How is this position evidenced in *The Handmaid's Tale*?
2. According to Atwood, "...writing is a gambler's profession. There is no guarantee of anything. You can put in a lot of time, a lot of effort, invest a great deal of emotional energy, and nothing may come out of it." How do you think this relates to Offred's writing and the effects it may have had on Gilead? Do you think that she would have considered herself a writer? Why or why not?

More

Examples of Literary Techniques from the Novel
Analyze the author's use of literary techniques and how they contribute to the narrative of *The Handmaid's Tale*.

1. Choose one literary technique used in the novel. In what particular way did the author use this literary technique? How effective was its usage?
2. What arguments can be made for the use of your chosen literary technique in a text? If this technique were overused or underutilized, what effect might it have on an author's work?

Theme in the Novel

The theme of a story is the underlying topic, idea, or position. It is often a general, universal statement about life. Sometimes, the theme is clearly stated, and other times, it is merely suggested. A theme is different from the topic of a novel. While a topic is the overall subject of a novel, a theme makes a statement about the topic in question. Theme can be expressed through the events that take place in the story, the ideas repeated along the way, and the lessons characters learn. Themes are often open to interpretation. A reader may have to examine many different aspects of a novel to form an opinion about its themes.

Values

Closely related to the novel's themes are the values held by the characters. The way in which characters act, react, and respond to the world around them helps unveil the themes and values of the characters, author, and story. Sometimes, these values will inform or become the basis of a particular theme in the novel.

Major Themes of *The Handmaid's Tale*

A major theme in *The Handmaid's Tale* is the power of language and naming. While the Gilead regime controls women's bodies and their roles, Offred rebels by naming herself and her situation. The novel also focuses on religion and **theocracy**. Using the Bible as justification, Gilead turns women's bodies into one of its political instruments. As Atwood says, "It does seem to be that every **totalitarian** government on the planet has always taken a very great interest in women's reproductive rights."

Language and Naming

"My name isn't Offred, I have another name, which nobody uses now because it's forbidden. I tell myself it doesn't matter, your name is like your telephone number, useful only to others; but what I tell myself is wrong, it does matter. I keep the knowledge of this name like something hidden, some treasure I'll come back to dig up, one day. I think of this name as buried. This name has an aura around it, like an amulet, some charm that's survived from an unimaginably distant past."

Offred, Chapter Fourteen

Offred

ACTIVITIES

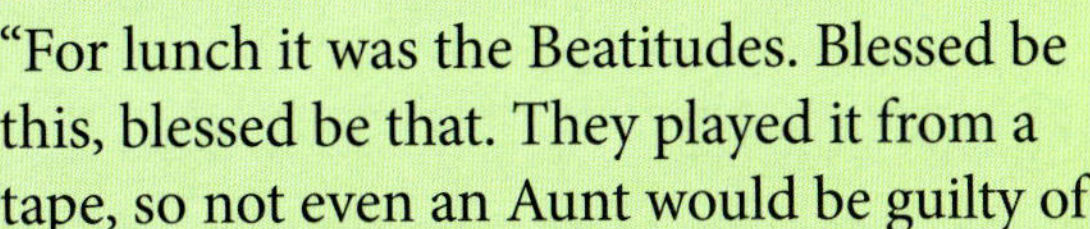

Offred

Religion and Theocracy

"For lunch it was the Beatitudes. Blessed be this, blessed be that. They played it from a tape, so not even an Aunt would be guilty of the sin of reading. The voice was a man's. *Blessed be the poor in spirit, for theirs is the kingdom of heaven. Blessed are the merciful. Blessed are the meek. Blessed are the silent.* I knew they made that up, I knew it was wrong, and they left things out too, but there was no way of checking. *Blessed be those that mourn, for they shall be comforted.*
Nobody said when."

Offred, Chapter Fifteen

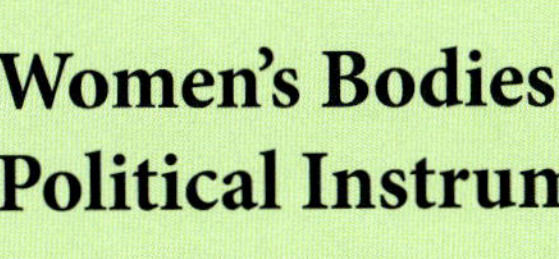

Women's Bodies as Political Instruments

"It's forbidden for us to be alone with the Commanders. We are for breeding purposes: we aren't concubines, geisha girls, courtesans. On the contrary: everything possible has been done to remove us from that category... We are two-legged wombs, that's all: sacred vessels, **ambulatory chalices**."

Offred, Chapter Twenty-Three

Secondary Themes

Secondary themes work with a novel's major themes to help the reader understand the narrative and characters. Atwood's secondary themes reinforce her major themes. The theme of women and children, including the inability of many women to bear children, underscores the importance of the political role of women's bodies. Another example of a secondary theme is the way people react to the gradually increasing oppression by their culture and government. As Offred says, "We lived as usual by ignoring...Nothing changes instantaneously: in a gradually heating bathtub, you'd be boiled to death before you knew it."

Weblink

What is Theme, and Why is it Important?
Evaluate the article discussing what theme is and why it matters.

1. The writer of the article gives a working definition of theme as "[a]n idea, concept, or lesson that appears repeatedly throughout a story, reflects the character's internal journey through the external plot, and resonates with the reader." Do you think that the themes of *The Handmaid's Tale* fit this definition? If so, provide specific examples to support your position. If not, how would you modify this definition to better fit the themes of the novel?
2. According to the writer of the article, "[i]f a story lacks theme, the reader might not connect with it." How do the themes Atwood uses help readers to connect with Offred's story?

More

Major and Secondary Themes
Analyze the author's development of themes over the course of the novel.

1. Choose a secondary theme from this spread and analyze its appearances in the novel. How does this theme first emerge? Which is the most poignant example of this theme in the novel?
2. What particular commentary might the author be making about life as a result of this theme's presence in the text? Explain and defend your ideas.
3. Choose a major theme presented on pages 16–17. In what ways does your chosen secondary theme relate to this major theme? Does it deepen or detract from the major theme? How or in what way?

RUBRIC

Creating a Symbolism Poster

Students will choose one of the other symbols listed on page 19 and analyze its role in the novel. They will then create a poster to present their analysis. An exemplary symbolism poster will meet the following criteria.

- Presents a clear purpose that is conveyed throughout the poster
- Shows an understanding of the concept of symbolism and the role it has in the novel
- Provides an in-depth analysis of what the symbol represents
- Discusses the role the symbol has in the novel
- Clearly indicates where the symbol appears in the novel
- Uses specific, detailed examples from the text to support the analysis
- Makes clear connections to the text
- Properly integrates all quotations
- Organizes the information in a logical, easy-to-read manner
- Includes high-quality graphics that relate to the symbol and effectively enhance understanding of the topic
- Features clear and concise writing
- Uses correct spelling, grammar, and punctuation
- Clearly labels items of importance
- Headings and subheadings are clear and easy to read
- Uses layout to creatively enhances the information
- Creates a poster that is attractive in terms of layout, design, and organization
- Shows a strong effort by the student

Symbolism in the Novel

A symbol is a person, place, action, or thing that stands for something beyond itself. A **tangible** concept, a symbol represents an intangible thing. Writers use symbolism to create a specific mood or emotion in a story. Symbols often gain meaning and strength if they are repeated throughout a story. Their meaning can change throughout the book. When studying a work of literature, the reader can gain a deeper understanding of the story by identifying and analyzing the writer's symbols.

Red as a Symbol

Atwood uses many different symbols throughout *The Handmaid's Tale*. The color red permeates the book. The Handmaids' clothing is red, suggesting blood, passion, and fertility. Gilead is obsessed with the Handmaids' ability to bear children, sending them for monthly checkups with a doctor. Red is also a symbol of sin. The Commanders' wives view the Handmaids, who bore children before the time of Gilead, as sinful. The flowers in Serena Joy's garden are red, becoming darker near the stem, as if healing from a cut. A red Birthmobile takes the Handmaids to a birthing.

The Color Red

"I get up out of the chair, advance my feet into the sunlight, in their red shoes, flat-heeled to save the spine and not for dancing. The red gloves are lying on the bed. I pick them up, pull them onto my hands, finger by finger. Everything except the wings around my face is red: the colour of blood, which defines us. The skirt is ankle-length, full, gathered to a flat yoke that extends over the breasts, the sleeves are full. The white wings too are prescribed issue; they are to keep us from seeing, but also from being seen. I never looked good in red, it's not my colour."

Offred, Chapter Two

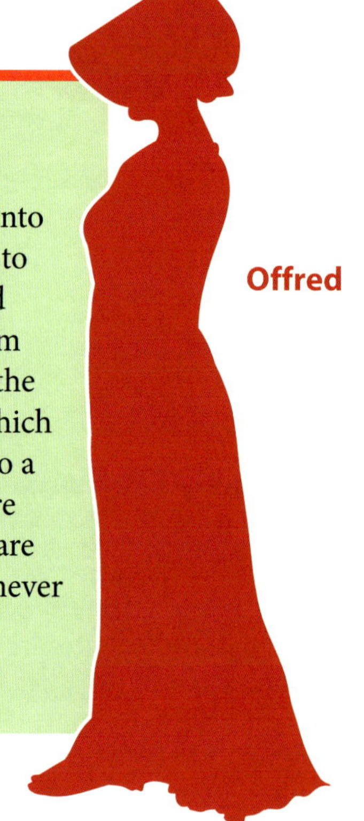

Offred

What Symbols Appear in the Novel?

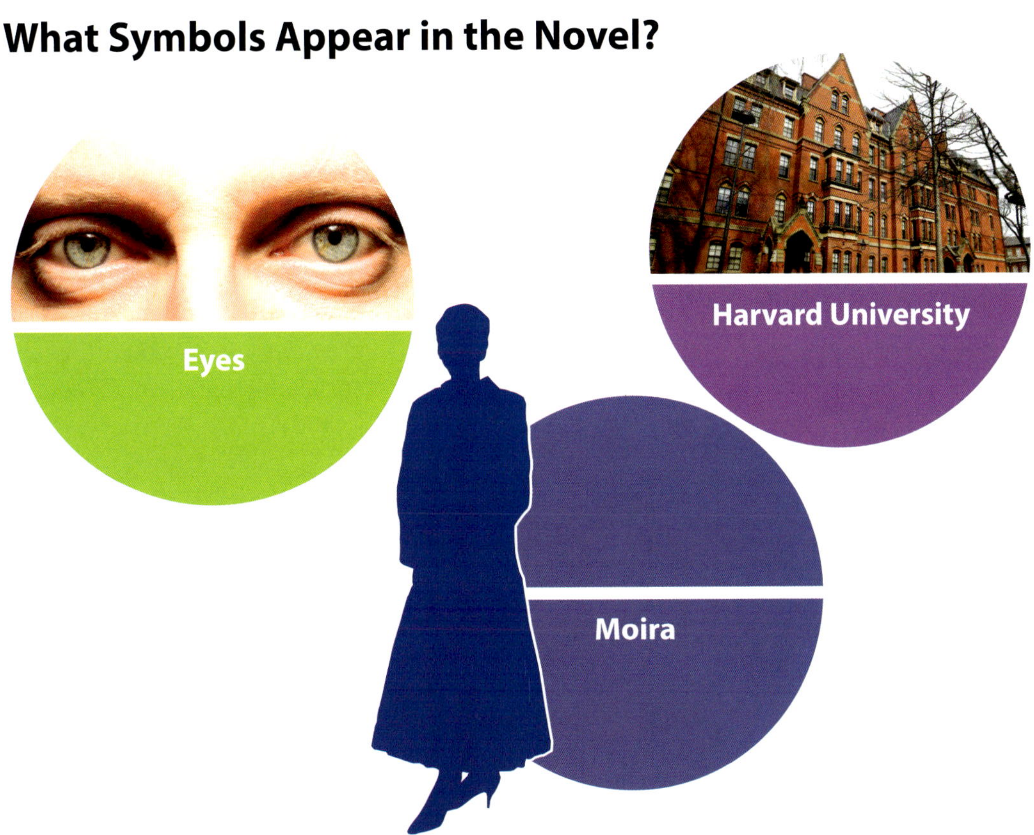

ACTIVITIES

 **More**

What Symbols Appear in the Novel?
Assess the author's use of symbolism in the novel.

1. Choose an example from the chart and analyze what this symbol represents. For which character is this symbol the most poignant in the novel? For which character is the symbol least poignant? Argue your opinions with clear reasons.
2. How is this symbol used or reflected in the novel's themes? Illustrate the ways in which the author's use of language deepens or weakens the meaning of the symbol. Explain and defend your ideas.

Weblink

The Complete Guide to Symbolism
Examine the blog post discussing the usage of symbolism in literature.

1. Contrast and compare examples of analytical descriptions of feelings and sensory descriptions using symbolism from the novel. Which kind is more effective in the novel? Provide reasons for your ideas.
2. Should analytical descriptions play a considerable role in the language of a novel? Why or why not?

Other Symbols in the Novel

Eyes

Eyes in Gilead are a symbol of the state and its intrusion into citizens' lives. The Eyes are the government's spies, both on the street, and perhaps in Offred's house, as Ofglen suggests. Black vans with a winged Eye painted on the side represent both the watchfulness of the state and the eternal eye of God focused on the world. People disappear into these vans, and the reader does not know what becomes of them.

Harvard University

Harvard University becomes a symbol of how the Gilead regime has turned the city of Cambridge and the rest of New England upside down. Once a place of learning and freedom, it is now where the Eyes work to suppress thought.

Moira

Moira is a symbol of freedom and daring to Offred and the other Handmaids. Her escape from the Red Center represents the possibility that they, too, could be free. Moira almost escapes into Canada on the Underground Femaleroad. When she is captured, the regime gives her a spirit-breaking choice. She can clean up toxic waste in the colonies, a deadly job, or go to work at Jezebel's. Moira is transformed into a symbol of the lack of options for infertile women.

RUBRIC

Analyzing a Video

Students will watch and assess a video related to a component of the novel, and write an analysis of the video. An exemplary video analysis will meet the following criteria.

- Identifies the purpose of the video
- Identifies the intended audience of the video
- Describes how the content of the video is presented
- Summarizes the information and opinions presented in the video
- Analyzes the quality of the content presented in the video
- Assesses the effectiveness of the video
- Discusses the technical aspects of the video and whether or not these enhance the content
- Determines whether the images and graphics used in the video relate to the content
- Determines whether the video is easy to follow and understand
- Gives the analysis a clear and consistent purpose
- Organizes the analysis in a logical, effective manner
- Presents a strong, clear argument about the video
- Provides strong and accurate details to support the argument about the video
- Considers other perspectives on the purpose and effectiveness of the video
- Makes connections between the video and the novel
- Properly integrates quotations from the video
- Cites all sources used in the analysis

The Use of Language

In *The Handmaid's Tale*, language is deadly serious, something that someone can be killed over, but also playful. One way that Atwood plays with words is in her creation of new words, which are often portmanteau words, or two words or parts of words joined together to create a new meaning.

The Gilead regime also plays with words, making up new meanings for old words, such as "Salvaging" and "Marthas." A "Salvaging" is now a large-scale execution, while Marthas are basically household servants. The regime also creates new words from bits of old ones, such as "Particicution," a brutal form of execution.

The Transformation of Language

The language of *The Handmaid's Tale* changes dramatically in the Historical Notes section, where a history professor who studies the Gilead period lectures his audience. The reader can **infer** from this that the Gilead regime has ended, and from the language he uses, the reader can see that the professor is smug, self-satisfied, and somewhat patriarchal. The professor does not indict Gilead and its reduction of women to their fertility status, but instead, tells his audience of the pressures the society was under.

While Gilead tries to silence women, Professor Pieixoto follows suit, ironically and to a lesser extent. He treats the narrator and her story as a historical curiosity instead of the report of a real person. Her communication to the reader and the future is regarded as suspect and of less value than that of a man. Pieixoto wishes she had been a spy or a reporter exploring the workings of Gilead, and exclaims to his audience, "What would we not give, now, for even twenty pages or so of print-out from Waterford's private computer!"

The Use of Quotation Marks

Atwood uses quotation marks to both challenge and alert the reader. Quotation marks show dialogue as it happens in reality. Without quotation marks, speech becomes mixed with thoughts and memories, so the reader must then interpret the multiple meanings of the text.

"I tell, therefore you are."

"I used to think of my body as an instrument, of pleasure, or a means of transportation, or an implement for the accomplishment of my will."

"Kick in the door, and what did I tell you? Caught in the act, sinfully Scrabbling. Quick, eat those words."

"That is what you have to do before you kill, I thought. You have to create an it, where none was before."

"When power is scarce, a little of it is tempting."

"Moira was like an elevator with open sides. She made us dizzy."

"...I'm only having an attack of sentimentality, my brain going pastel."

"I smell a rat. Misfit as odor."

"Sometimes these flashes of normality come at me from the side, like ambushes. The ordinary, the usual, a reminder, like a kick."

"The sitting room is subdued, symmetrical; it's one of the shapes money takes when it freezes."

ACTIVITIES

Video

Handmaids Tale Part 2: Crash Course Literature #404

Learn more about why Atwood presents the final section of the novel from the perspective of a male scholar by watching this video.

1. In the video, John Green observes that "it was male editors who created the structure to Offred's narrative that we're reading." How might this be viewed as problematic? Why do you think Atwood included this detail in the story? What effect does this fact have on the reader's interpretation of the novel?
2. John posits that Pieixoto "may fancy himself above the injustices of Gilead." Do you consider Pieixoto to be above these injustices, as he likely believes himself to be? Why or why not?
3. John refers to the "tremendous value in the way that Offred has told her story." What is this value, and why might readers recognize it while Pieixoto does not?

Weblink

Under His eye: prescriptive language and *The Handmaid's Tale*

Explore some of the prescriptive language used in the novel by reading this blog post.

1. What is the connection between the salutations used in *The Handmaid's Tale* and the Bible? Do all of the residents of Gilead use these greetings for the same reasons? Explain your answer.
2. What is the significance of the term "Marthas"? Why do you think Atwood chose this name?

RUBRIC

Writing a Review

Students will write a review of the novel. An exemplary review will meet the following criteria.

- Grabs the reader's attention with a creative headline
- Begins with an engaging lead to pull the reader into the article
- Introduces the title of the novel, the author, and the genre
- Provides a brief plot description that does not give away the entire story, and makes the reader want to learn more about the novel
- Supports arguments about the novel with accurate and detailed information
- Organizes the review and its arguments in a concise, clear, and logical manner
- Fits the format and style of a review
- Follows the conventions of print or online journalism
- Demonstrates creativity in their approach
- Writes with a unique, engaging voice and perspective
- Provides fresh insight into the novel
- Provides an honest, authentic opinion on the novel
- Gives a clear recommendation on the novel, backed up by specific textual evidence
- Uses correct spelling, grammar, and punctuation

Impact of the Novel at the Time of Publishing

At the time of publication, reviewers focused on two main questions regarding *The Handmaid's Tale*. They asked, did the society and government that Atwood described work plausibly, and was *The Handmaid's Tale* a success as literature? Some reviewers considered it well written, but implausible, and thought far-right conservatives would never be able to establish a government based on religion. Others found it all-too realistic, and based on political and cultural events of the time. Many reviewers agreed, however, that it was a fascinating read.

Three Nations' Reactions

Atwood describes three different reactions to the book at publication. Great Britain had already endured a religious civil war and could not imagine another one, so British readers thought it was a "jolly good yarn." Atwood portrays her native Canada as an ever-anxious country, where the reaction was, "Could it happen here?" In contrast, the U.S. response was "How long have we got?" Atwood explains, "So even then, in 1985, people were feeling quite alarmed about some of the things in the book. And they also were saying things like well, you know, is this about the Middle East? And I would say it's actually no, it's about everybody."

Awards and Recognition

The Handmaid's Tale won the Governor-General's Award for the best Canadian fiction written in English in 1985. In 1987, it won the annual Arthur C. Clarke award, a British award given for the best science fiction novel first published in the United Kingdom. In 1986, it was also shortlisted for the Man Booker Prize, the leading literary award in the English-speaking world. That same year, the novel was also nominated for a Nebula award.

ACTIVITIES

Banning the Book

From 1990 to 1999, *The Handmaid's Tale* was listed as 37th of the top 100 most-banned books. Often, parents wanted to ban the book from high schools for being profane, sexually explicit, and violently graphic, and also claimed it **denigrated** minorities, God, women, and the disabled. Defenders said that the controversy surrounding the book indicated its quality and significance. Atwood noted that when a book was banned, its sales increased, claiming, "If it's a book with any power, there's always going to be some sort of uproar."

Atwood's Expectations

When Atwood first wrote *The Handmaid's Tale*, she knew that the book's controversial subject matter would likely polarize readers. She had concerns about showing the book to an editor, so Atwood decided to have a friend read a draft first, commenting, "I think I'm going to get a lot of hate mail." After reading the draft, her friend responded with the prediction, "I think you're going to be rich."

Since its publication **in 1985**, *The Handmaid's Tale* has **never been out of print**.

The book was originally titled **Offred**, after the main character.

The Handmaid's Tale was on the list of the **top 100 banned books** of the decade in the 1990s and 2000s.

Document

The New York Times Book Review of The Handmaid's Tale

Analyze the review by Mary McCarthy, published on February 9, 1986, exploring her views on *The Handmaid's Tale*.

1. What is the tone of the review? Why does McCarthy describe *The Handmaid's Tale* as "a poet's novel"? Is this a fair assessment? Why or why not?
2. According to McCarthy, if the novel "doesn't scare one, doesn't wake one up, it must be because it has no satiric bite." Do you agree with this assertion? Defend your opinion with solid arguments.

Weblink

What Critics Said About 'The Handmaid's Tale' Back In The 1980s

Find out more about the novel's initial critical reception in this *Huffington Post* article by Claire Fallon, published on April 13, 2017.

1. Fallon claims that "[t]he concept of a dystopia premised on the theocratic oppression of women, perhaps unsurprisingly, has always been polarizing." Why do you think this is the case?
2. Which of the three categories of reviews cited in the article align most closely with your opinions on the novel? Why? What makes you disagree with the reviews from the other two categories?

Impact of the Novel Now

The book continues to be both powerful and controversial today. As Atwood wrote in 2012, "Some books haunt the reader. Others haunt the writer. *The Handmaid's Tale* has done both."

Political Protests

Soon after the 2016 U.S. presidential election, sales of both *The Handmaid's Tale* and George Orwell's dystopian novel *1984* soared. References to *The Handmaid's Tale* became more frequent, especially at political events. Women dressed in red gowns and white bonnets appeared at legislative meetings and rallies, protesting laws increasing restrictions to women's access to reproductive health care. At protest marches after the 2017 inauguration, some people carried signs saying, "*The Handmaid's Tale* is not an instruction manual."

40 *The Handmaid's Tale* has been **translated** into **40** or **more** languages.

Already an **opera** and a **ballet**, *The Handmaid's Tale* is also being made into a **graphic novel** in **2018**.

A **film adaptation** of the novel **was released** in **1990**.

Atwood's Role Today

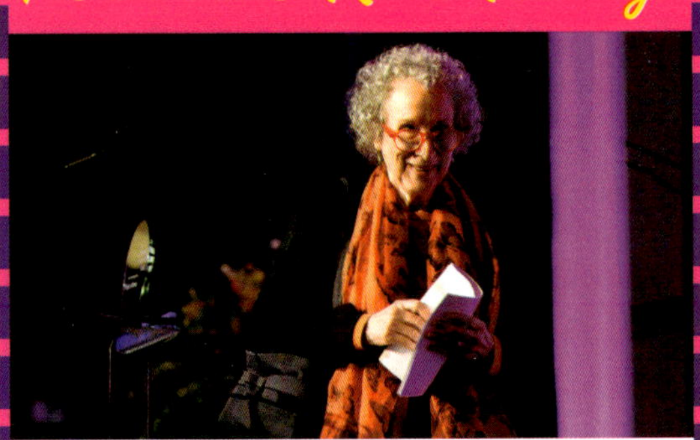

In 2017, Atwood received lifetime achievement awards from the National Book Critics Circle and from one of the world's oldest literary organizations, PEN Center USA. She speaks out frequently about the U.S. political climate, and is also involved in the second season of the Hulu series adaptation of the book, inventing the future of Offred, other major characters, and Gilead itself. Atwood has had more than thirty years to think about what happens next in the world of *The Handmaid's Tale*.

Streaming Success

In 2017, the streaming service Hulu released its first season of a series titled *The Handmaid's Tale*. While staying close to the novel in most ways, it also updates it with modern technology such as smartphones, and Uber, a private car-hiring company. A dramatic change from the book was including actors of color in major roles. In the original novel, African Americans were shipped to the Midwest. Jewish people were allowed to convert to Christianity or sent to Israel, but they were not seen on the streets of Gilead. The show won the 2017 Emmy for outstanding drama series.

New Updates

A new recording of the novel released in 2017 contains additional details, including an extended Historical Notes section. In the new version, when the professor invites questions, queries and answers follow. When asked what might encourage a new Gilead to arise, he answers, "environmental stresses that lead to food shortages, economic factors such as unrest due to unemployment, a social structure that is top-heavy, with too much wealth being concentrated among too few." He also notes how **propaganda** would change, saying "If there is no true news, false news can be made very plausible."

ACTIVITIES

Video

In dystopian 'Handmaid's Tale,' a warning for a new generation not to take rights for granted
Learn more about the production of the Hulu adaptation of Atwood's novel by watching this video.

1. In the video, Atwood says that she "gets in trouble" when she tries to make a distinction between science fiction and speculative fiction. Why do you think this is the case? Do you believe this is an important distinction to make?
2. Executive producer Warren Littlefield and showrunner/screenwriter Bruce Miller point out that the show's writing staff is made up predominantly of women, and that four out of five of its directors are women. Why is this so important when it comes to telling this particular story?

Document

The Visceral, Woman-Centric Horror of *The Handmaid's Tale*
Analyze the review by Sophie Gilbert, published on April 25, 2017, exploring her views on the Hulu adaptation of *The Handmaid's Tale*.

1. It is noted that this adaptation "retains Offred's inner monologue." Why do you think this decision was made? What might the effect have been if the creators of the show did not do this? Why do you think so?
2. In Gilbert's opinion, the onscreen relationship between Serena Joy and Offred "sheds light on the question of how the story relates to contemporary womanhood, with its questions of intersectionality and white feminism." What does this mean to you? Explain your answer.

RUBRIC

Creating a Timeline

Students will explore a topic related to the novel and create a timeline to present their research on historical events connected to this topic. An exemplary timeline will meet the following criteria.

- Includes the most significant events pertaining to the topic to be compared and analyzed
- Includes interesting events
- Uses accurate information for all events, including date, location, and major details
- Orders the events in a chronological sequence
- Describes each event with accurate, vivid, and specific details
- Presents the topic from three or more perspectives
- Inspires the reader to ask thoughtful questions regarding the events and perspectives presented in the timeline
- Uses correct spelling, grammar, and punctuation
- Presents the timeline in a visually attractive and striking manner
- Presents the timeline in a neat, organized manner that is logical and easy to follow
- Uses creativity to present the timeline in an engaging manner
- Effectively communicates the historical information relating to the topic
- Supports each event with reliable sources
- Expresses a clear purpose for creating the timeline
- Enhances the reader's understanding of the topic
- Includes a correctly formatted bibliography of all sources used to create the timeline

Perspectives on Women's Rights

This twentieth-century novel explores many twenty-first-century concerns. These include environmental destruction, artificial viruses, the dangers of nuclear power, the abuses of power, sexism, racism, and homophobia. Gilead is presented as a step back in terms of human development.

Timeline of Women's Rights

1769 The American colonies adopt the British common law, which did not allow married women to own property or keep their own earnings.

1918 Margaret Sanger wins a lawsuit in New York allowing doctors to tell their married patients about birth control for health purposes. The clinic joins with others to become Planned Parenthood in 1942.

1700s

1800s

1920 The Nineteenth Amendment to the U.S. Constitution is officially approved, ensuring the right of women to vote.

1848 The Seneca Falls Convention issues a plea for the end of discrimination against women and launches the women's **suffrage** movement.

1964 Title VII of the Civil Rights Act passes Congress, forbidding discrimination on the basis of sex in employment. The Equal Employment Opportunity Commission is created.

One predominant theme in *The Handmaid's Tale* is the loss of women's rights. Currently, fundamentalist religious movements in some countries, such as Afghanistan, are depriving girls of the right to education. In other countries, cultural attitudes keep girls from attending school. In the United States, laws restricting women's rights often center around access to health care and birth control.

1900s

1972 The U.S. Supreme Court upholds unmarried couples' right to use birth controls.

1973 In Roe v. Wade, the U.S. Supreme Court rules that abortion is legal.

1984 Geraldine Ferraro becomes the first female to be nominated to be vice president of the United States on a major party ticket.

1992 Record numbers of women are elected to Congress, with 4 women winning Senate seats and 24 women elected to first terms in the House.

1994 Congress passes the Violence Against Women Act. Among its provisions, it ensures funding for services for victims of sexual assault and domestic violence. In 2000, the Supreme Court invalidates part of the act which gives victims of sexual assault and/or domestic violence the ability to sue their attackers for civil damages.

2000s

2016 Hillary Rodham Clinton becomes the first woman representing a major political party to run for president of the United States.

2017 Congress tries repeatedly to deny funding for any medical service of Planned Parenthood, including cancer screenings and birth control.

ACTIVITIES

Transparency–Timeline

Timeline of Women's Rights

Examine the historical and cultural contexts shown on the timeline. Then, contrast and correlate its elements with the themes and events presented in *The Handmaid's Tale.*

1. In what ways can historical events, culture, and social mores influence a population's perspective on women's rights? How might these elements have shaped the way a reader in the late 1980s interpreted the novel?
2. How might the era in which Margaret Atwood wrote *The Handmaid's Tale* have influenced the novel's themes and settings? Where in the novel is this most evident? Explain your reasoning.
3. Which current events, changes in laws, new ideas, or political discussions are shaping women's rights in the United States today? Which ideas and attitudes are still prevailing? Why?
4. How might current events and present perspectives affect the way a reader interprets the novel? Why is it important for readers to understand the era and context in which a novel is written?

RUBRIC

Writing a Comparative Essay

Students will compare two literary devices used in the novel, and then write a comparative essay based on their analysis. An exemplary comparative essay will meet the following criteria.

- Consists of a one-paragraph introduction, three body paragraphs, and a one-paragraph conclusion
- Introduction includes an engaging lead statement about the topic of the essay, more detailed information about the novel, and a one-sentence thesis that specifically states the essay's argument
- Body paragraphs include a topic sentence that refers to the thesis and how the idea appears in the novel, a supporting sentence that points to this part of the novel, textual evidence of this idea from the novel, and analysis of this evidence
- Body paragraphs end with a transition to the next paragraph
- Conclusion refers to the topic of the essay and the three points presented in the body paragraphs, and restates the thesis
- Provides a thorough analysis of the literary devices in question
- Cites strong and thorough textual evidence to support analysis of what the novel says explicitly
- Presents a clear, specific thesis that indicates a high level of critical engagement
- Organizes ideas in a logical manner
- Communicates arguments in a clear, effective manner
- Properly integrates all quotations
- Correctly cites all sources used
- Correctly formats bibliography

Writing a Comparative Essay

The Handmaid's Tale features one major character, who serves as both the narrator and protagonist. Offred tells her story and describes the rest of the characters. As such, readers only have her perspective on each of the characters and the dialogue she exchanges with them to inform their impressions. Choose two characters from the novel and make a list of their attributes. Compare and contrast the attributes of the two characters and decide how they are similar and different. Then, write an essay arguing your conclusion. Support your argument with logical reasoning and evidence from the novel.

How to Analyze and Compare Characters

Use the chart to guide your comparison of two characters in *The Handmaid's Tale.*

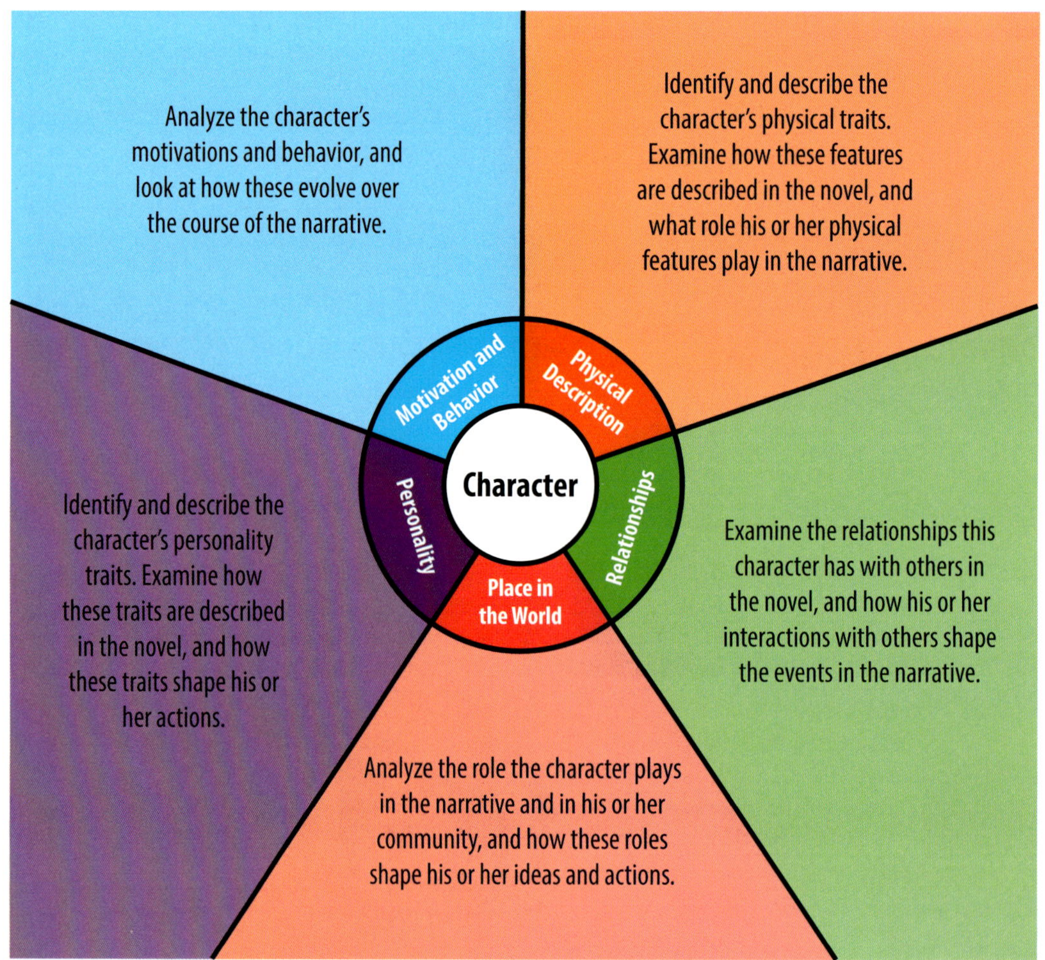

ACTIVITIES

Comparing Offred and the Commander

Offred

Place in the World
- Protagonist of the novel
- Educated
- Valued only for her fertility
- Was once an employee, mother, and wife, but no longer

Motivation and Behavior
- Is trying to survive in a terrifying new society
- Misses her former life
- Misses her child
- Wonders what happened to her husband and to Moira
- Contemplates stealing to offset her powerlessness as a Handmaid
- Has no control over her destiny
- Feels shame over her conduct toward Janine in the Red Center

Personality
- Intelligent
- Ironic
- Observant
- Enjoys having small moments of power

Relationships
- Loves her child
- Loves her husband
- Both resents and feels sorry for Serena Joy
- Physically attracted to Nick
- Misses her best friend, Moira

Physical Description
- Is fertile
- Is 33 years old
- Has brown hair
- Is 5 feet, 7 inches tall

Commander

Motivation and Behavior
- Is willing to take chances with other people's lives
- Rationalizes Gilead
- Values power over people

Physical Description
- Gray hair
- Looks "like a midwestern banker"
- Probably sterile

Place in the World
- Powerful man in Gilead
- Head of the household
- One of the antagonists in the novel
- Represents the banality of evil
- May be Frederick Waterford
- May have been a marketing specialist before Gilead

Relationships
- Difficult to know his relationships because reader only sees the Commander through Offred
- Enjoys power over Handmaids
- Once liked Serena Joy enough to marry her
- Feels his wife does not understand him and so justifies his dangerous relationship with Offred

Personality
- Lonely for intellectual stimulation from women
- Sexist
- Likes to read
- Rebellious against social rules
- Ingenious
- A hypocrite
- Condescending

More

Questions for Character Analysis

Analyze how specific character features, such as conflicts, motivations, relationships, place in the world, and personality affect the plot of *The Handmaid's Tale*. Cite strong and thorough textual evidence to support your analysis of what the novel says explicitly as well as the inferences you may have drawn from the novel's setting, themes, and symbols.

Quiz Answers

1. D
2. A
3. C
4. C
5. A
6. D
7. B
8. A
9. A
10. B

Key Words

ambulatory: able to walk

chalices: goblets, especially those used in the Christian ceremony of Communion

chronological: arranged in the order of time

denigrated: criticized and ridiculed unfairly

dystopian: describing an imaginary state where everything is unpleasant

entomologist: someone who studies insects

evangelism: the spreading of the Christian gospel by preaching or making a personal commitment to Christ

indoctrinate: to teach the beliefs of a specific group

infer: to derive a conclusion from information

infertile: unable to bear or beget children

propaganda: statements, not always accurate, intended to promote an idea, policy, or government

suffrage: the right to vote

tangible: something that can be assessed through the five senses

theocracy: a government in which the leaders are tied to the church or a specific religion. Leaders rule in the name of a god or gods

totalitarian: relating to a political system that requires its citizens to blindly follow the rules of the government, and that controls all aspects of life, including politics, economy, culture, religion, and the private lives of citizens

utopian: describing a place of perfection in terms of laws, government, and social conditions

Literary Terms

action: everything that occurs in a narrative

antagonist: the character who stands in opposition to the protagonist; in some cases, the antagonist creates or represents the conflict that the protagonist faces

climax: the moment of greatest tension in the story's action

conflict: a struggle between two or more opposing forces, creating a tension that must be resolved

dialogue: the spoken conversations that the characters have with each other

exposition: the beginning of the story, where the characters and setting are introduced

falling action: the events that take place after the climax, leading up to the end of the story

Freytag's Pyramid: a narrative structure consisting of five elements; this includes exposition, rising action, climax, falling action, and resolution

literary elements: components of every literary work

literary techniques: unique structures of a literary work

narrative: a logically arranged series of events presented for an audience; a story

narrator: the character or person telling the story, providing background information and opinions on the events, and connecting the gaps between major events and dialogue

plot: the specific action that propels a story forward

protagonist: the central character in a piece of fiction who must deal with a conflict and often undergoes some type of change as a result

resolution: the end of the story, when the problems are resolved and the action comes to a conclusion

rising action: the events that create increased drama or tension

symbolism: a stylistic device using symbols to represent and intensify concepts and ideas

Index

LIGHTBOX

SUPPLEMENTARY RESOURCES

Click on the plus icon found in the bottom left corner of each spread to open additional teacher resources.

- Download and print the book's quizzes and activities
- Access curriculum correlations
- Explore additional web applications that enhance the Lightbox experience

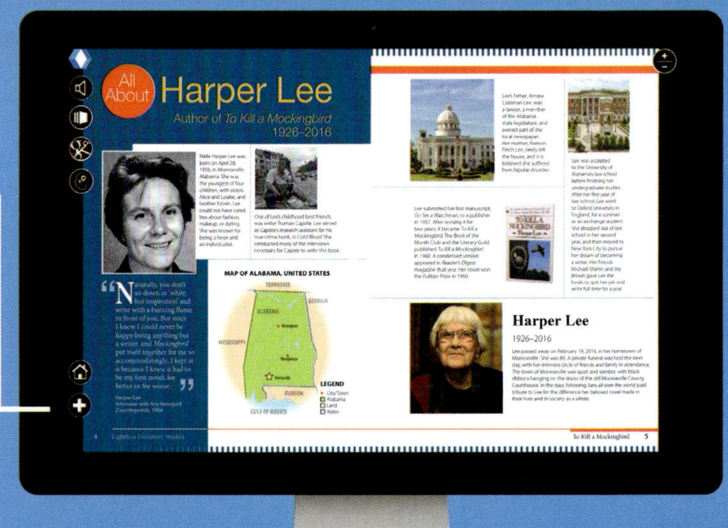

LIGHTBOX DIGITAL TITLES

Packed full of integrated media

VIDEOS

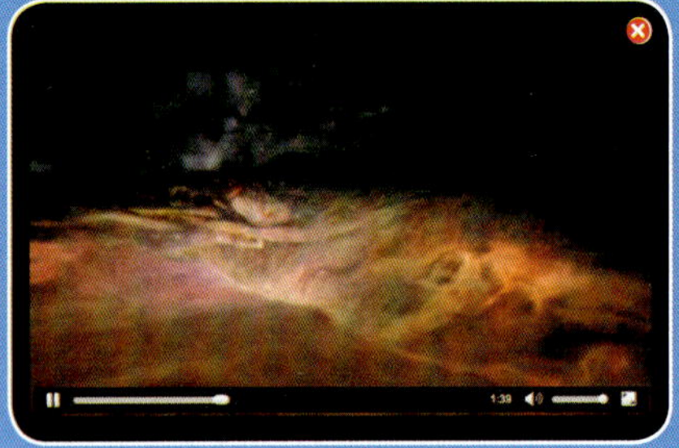

INTERACTIVE MAPS

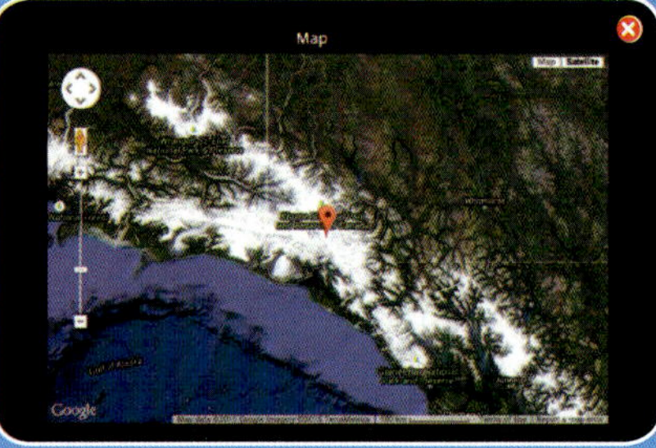

WEBLINKS

SLIDESHOWS

QUIZZES

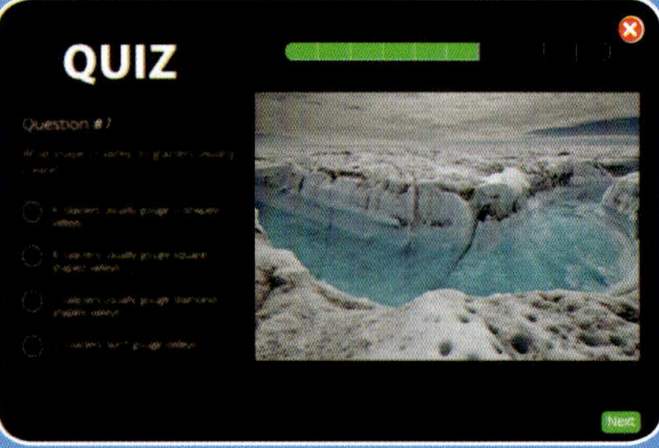

OPTIMIZED FOR

- ✓ TABLETS
- ✓ WHITEBOARDS
- ✓ COMPUTERS
- ✓ AND MUCH MORE!

Published by Smartbook Media Inc.
350 5th Avenue, 59th Floor New York, NY 10118
Website: www.openlightbox.com

Library of Congress Cataloging-in-Publication Data
Names: Weber, Valerie, author. | Gillespie, Katie, author.
Title: The handmaid's tale / Valerie Weber and Katie Gillespie..
Description: New York, NY : Smartbook Media Inc., [2018] | Series: Lightboxliterature studies | Includes index.
Identifiers: LCCN 2017054079 (print) | LCCN 2017056495 (ebook) | ISBN 9781510537033 (Muti-User eBook) | ISBN 9781510537026 (hard cover : alk.paper)
Subjects: LCSH: Atwood, Margaret, 1939- Handmaid's tale--Examinations--Studyguides. | Atwood, Margaret, 1939- Handmaid's tale--Juvenile literature.
Classification: LCC PR9199.3.A8 (ebook) | LCC PR9199.3.A8 H334 2018 (print) |DDC 813/.54--dc23
LC record available at https://lccn.loc.gov/2017054079

Printed in Brainerd, Minnesota, United States
1 2 3 4 5 6 7 8 9 0 22 21 20 19 18

052018
121017

Editor: Katie Gillespie
Art Director: Terry Paulhus

The publisher acknowledges Getty Images, iStock, and Alamy as its primary image suppliers for this title.